D0789268

OR TO BEGIN AGAIN

BOOKS WITH ARTISTS

Thripsis
(with Joe Brainard)

A Clown, Some Colors, A Doll, Her Stories,
A Song, A Moonlit Cove
(with Ellen Phelan)

How Things Bear Their Telling
(with Lucio Pozzi)

Greeks
(with Jan Groover and Bruce Boice)

Sacred Weather
(with Louisa Chase)

OR TO BEGIN AGAIN

ANN LAUTERBACH

PENGUIN POETS

PENGUIN BOOKS

Published by the Penguin Group
Penguin Group (USA) Inc., 375 Hudson Street, New York, New York 10014, U.S.A.
Penguin Group (Canada), 90 Eglinton Avenue East, Suite 700, Toronto, Ontario, Canada M4P 2Y3
(a division of Pearson Penguin Canada Inc.)
Penguin Books Ltd, 80 Strand, London WC2R 0RL, England
Penguin Ireland, 25 St Stephen's Green, Dublin 2, Ireland (a division of Penguin Books Ltd)
Penguin Group (Australia), 250 Camberwell Road, Camberwell, Victoria 3124, Australia
(a division of Pearson Australia Group Pty Ltd)
Penguin Books India Pvt Ltd, 11 Community Centre, Panchsheel Park, New Delhi - 110 017, India
Penguin Group (NZ), 67 Apollo Drive, Rosedale, North Shore 0632, New Zealand
(a division of Pearson New Zealand Ltd)
Penguin Books (South Africa) (Pty) Ltd, 24 Sturdee Avenue, Rosebank, Johannesburg 2196, South Africa

Penguin Books Ltd, Registered Offices:
80 Strand, London WC2R 0RL, England

First published in Penguin Books 2009

1   3   5   7   9   10   8   6   4   2

Page ix constitutes an extension of this copyright page.

LIBRARY OF CONGRESS CATALOGING-IN-PUBLICATION DATA

Lauterbach, Ann, ——.
Or to begin again / Ann Lauterbach.
p. cm. — (Penguin poets)
ISBN 978-0-14-311520-5
I. Title.
PS3562.A844O7 2009
811'.54—dc22   2008038414

Printed in the United States of America
Set in Minion
Designed by Ginger Legato

For Constance Kaine and Thomas Neurath
In memory of Nikos Stangos

ACKNOWLEDGMENTS

The author would like to express her thanks to the editors of the journals in which some of these poems, often in earlier versions, first appeared: *Atlanta Review, Bard Papers, Conjunctions, Dog Under Porch, GlitterPony, No: A Journal of the Arts, 6x6.* An earlier version of "Nothing to Say" was published by Belladonna Books, #85.

Also: continued gratitude and affection to Paul Slovak at Viking Penguin; and to Lourdes Lopez and Anna Moschkovatis for their generous guidance and help; and to my colleagues and students at Bard College, for providing a buoyant community of inquiry and response.

A NOTE TO THE READER:
When a proper name appears in parenthesis after a title, it often indicates that the poem has been drawn from an encounter; notations written as I walked through an exhibition, or listened to someone give a talk; or from my reading of an essay or poem. Throughout this collection, I am interested in differences between spoken utterance and written text.

CONTENTS

I.

II.

III.

I.

The way of life is wonderful; it is by abandonment.

—EMERSON, "CIRCLES"

BIRD (THOREAU)

1.

The great stalks are alert, their
shambles piled: maybe another parade.

An evident gray, a slow march
and legions rudderless; an ordinary flow.

These none of them quite real, none present,
like mischief in a dream: the blue garment, the rusty blade.

Came late or have you come late or are you, you are late
then on into wakened sobriety's itch.

The great stalks move slightly. They press back.
Waiting folds upward into a shape

to be seen later, or not seen, not now, not later.
Take hold of this garment, this was said.

The thrust of these injunctions. *Take hold of the blade.*

2.

Stepping man is stiff in the shade.
Let him be, or chop him down.

At the far side of the miserable hill
an orchestra is rehearsing for the factory's ball.

As usual, a train is near, but there are no feet.
The wheels peel off into global dust

and there is flesh, naked flesh, exposed to it.
Where were you? asks stepping man.

Where are we? you answer, taking shelter.
In the other, invisible mode I glimpsed him

walking away, toward the river, into a meadow.
The head of stepping man is bowed. He

seems to be alone in history, alone in the brush.

3.

Stepping man: cowed, immobile, an
invention of the nude season; an invention of

new arrivals and the one tulip and
beating of the woman with a baseball bat.

He stepped on her face.
Hear these enactments

or forgo them in their temporal settings.
The material of the world? Will?

How the Jesuit and the young woman
might have walked along an avenue in 1960

and then, this long, this far away
in the tangle of the bare, emergent copse.

Stepping man recalls Thoreau and is envious.

4.

Drab us; lonely *sequitur.* Stepping man, distilled,
no more than a fake. Quaint acquisition, no

more than material fiction
to see or not to see. He

cannot look up, and the light
drifts across his shoulders

as the river slinks on to curse
his rigid stride:

New York, Albany, Troy, then
night and the music he might have known.

Stepping man, burning ash, the bird's
quick target—*carries the sky on its back.*

Dear Blank

The instant quarantine on its shelf.
Deletion ranged upward, proto-winged,
enough to go on, as if singular.
To then, if it were then
it looks like you are writing a letter
interrupts Knowledge, whose source cannot
be owned. Try not to fall apart.
Try to stay on the case, in case you need to fall
into speech, example, *It looks like you are writing
a letter.* To whom it may concern.
To be then concerned.

And so the unobserved passes through its glass
twilight. Hitched to its seam,
a spectacle tangles with a spider
caught among settings, conquests.
Nowhere does the announcement flair,
nowhere does the exception pertain.
The refrain, its indifference and scorn,
travels into the familiar trace of the already consumed.
Abstraction, the stagnant sign, becomes a wager.

And yet, one wants to say *and yet,*
night will come down over the water
and the train will approach its final destination.
She will turn her attention to leisure—
the good car, the good china, the good rosé.
Some eccentric ground will form under the atmosphere
where the bones lie, where the burned books
nourish the lilac. She will recall a friend's comment,
It looks like you are writing a letter.
Would you like help?

Others escaped. They will not sign their names.
They will stay for a while on a Greek island
while a child is conceived in another country.
She will say that its name must be pronounced
the same in French as in English
in the vicinity of the letter, in the habit of grace,
like, or unlike, the disinterested bird.

And so the generic is elicited from under the hood
along with anything winged, or sudden,
small in its habit and domain.
Witnessing the close, collecting the stuff,
counting the days until
what is pronounced comes into view
as a picture of a criminal or a lover or a child.
Remember? What was the name?
Dear Dick, Dear Pris, Dear Jen, Dear Tom.

ANTS IN THE SUGAR (BLANCHOT/MALLARMÉ)

1.

She puts the beginning into moist stuff, vague but substantial
among attributes. She puts the beginning in
as thought or as dream
but not to be praised or worked over,
not to be given to enterprise. She puts it in.
Something closes around it.

What then? Tireless, flamboyant sequence.
Guards running beside the car
like so many fish tagging a whale's belly,
a girl shines and flips like a coin,
goldfinches loop
among branches of crab apple.

Nature not at all present
and the present not present
at any beginning.

                    Quickening, surrender,

failure and omission coincident
what rots out a trophy scent
trots out its song

                    phantom aptitude

for which there is only a parade
moving through its sleeve
bringing the last to the first
parting the ritual valve

coming farther out

into the mere field
one leans back on the field
as if it were a wall

leans asking

Who is at the helm?
Who is leading this astray?
Who is behind the wall?

Who has bagged the plot

has issued forth the command
taken the recipient from the prize
canceled the flight
mocked the apparition of time
as not necessity, not damage, not a call

who nags

exposed to the sky
not to disclose its departure
nor its initial tug

as if it were a wall of light

flipping waves onto our links
as error illumines small white marks
enfolding the circus:
trails of dark ephemera
hasty attachment to the real.

2.

Baffled: where is the beginning, how will it open?
Not to anyone, a daisy or the various
   floods over and above
         the diaristic song
                  zones of retrieval
                  masked onto names

                        to say *hurry now hurry*
                  from the rude gaps of wind
                           cloistered by the throat

                           the vigilant stem

         arousal from stupor   lifting its head
              to be silenced and to begin again

                  rhythmic shelter *hello*
                        echoes
                              hello

   Who and who is listening?

                  Provision gripped
                  loosened from its tether
                  most narrow abatement

along the slope of the sound's appraisal
                  what was heard

         in the sanctity of the inner ear: w/ a/ e/ r

                we

                        are

                                we
                we   wear
                        war

                echo

so feeble as to be
enchanted

                if it were to return as itself
                if it were to respond

                that which repeats

                        I told you so
                                at risk of beginning

                        as if stepping across a bridge
                        where there is no bridge

                        sending a note
                        when there is nothing of note.

3.

Ants in the sugar.
I am waiting to calm down.
Ants in the sugar.
I am hoping to exit this stratum.

Who is that man walking along the road?
Who is that young girl in the pink dress?
Ants in the sugar.

4.

Foregrounding a static molecule.
Spectral instant.
Maybe something is arrested, maybe
an elemental marker but not as yet present.
Could wander away? Could be at last lost?
The steps, the path,
filtered through the single static molecule,
did they come through passages of debt,
coming back across the field, avoiding the story?
Through the blue glass and across the nodding limbs,
dragging its shadow but staggering nevertheless:
accurate zombie with a license to foretell.

Logic in ordinary garb approaches.
Not dissimilar to a job offer, or a court decision.
Also not a simple ordinance or sequence
on the lap, in the garden, after the initial hurrah.
Moon quest arrives in late twilight; moon quest
announces another go-round under the tutelage of sound,
ever sweet, ever persuasive in rendition.
The moon and the piano in accord,
as if distilled from smoke, a
pale yellow suspended in a pale blue.
Some darker visual incidents, some stray sounds.
Nature not present. Moon not present, not as moon.

5.

Feed the acid-loving plants.
Imagine the future.
Ants in the sugar.
That craft might collide with being, being
with others. That the blood might inhale toxins.

These, others: for example, the *this* or the *that*.
That she would withdraw, and the thing
would stink. That the body would exaggerate its claims
with its routines, its vitamins, its hurt ensemble.
That the cat would die in her arms.
That they would rush to the river to see the sunset.
That the dead girl's father would offer stones for the cairn.
That the instant would contain precision.
That the iris could be a definition.
That the shape of things to come would take another shape.
That the invention of the end is linguistic.

For Charlotte Mandell

Indictment without Subject

From the bourgeoisie tribe an aspect of looking.
The near settles in.
The near is rejected by the bourgeoisie tribe.
The bourgeoisie tribe
settles among its kinsmen
and adds to itself.

It watches the wasp struggle in bleach.
It erects implausible glass.
It brings into view the hanging man.
It enjoys the spectacle.
It copies out the printed day.

The bourgeoisie tribe makes babies.
The babies cry *I want*.
The babies cry *more*.
This is how it learns to count.

The roses are already in the fire.
The despot has been abased.
The shelter has been committed to film.
Weathers have reduced the population of herring.
Statements are made from
statements that have been made.
It, the tribe, is small among acts,
invisible from the erased horizon.
The sky is purring, engorged.
Steel has been seen to melt.
Steel with the strength of mutants and despots
has been seen to melt.
The articulating angel mauls the insentient thing.
The thing, a fiasco of nearness, erupts.

It seems to know fire; it seems to collapse
into whatever is without conversion,
no hand nor orifice, no babble, no touch.
It takes its place outside of the near.
The near comes on in, dragging a map.

NOTHING TO SAY

I have nothing to say and I am saying it.
— JOHN CAGE

1.

What? The other side? Now?
Not exactly, but what cannot be underlined or condemned.

This one for example, the fog and the police car sitting in the browning grass, cat asleep under the table. Thomas phones from London talking about Con's newly inherited Biedermeier furnishings

another

hurrying across the path, now stymied, which way the wind blows, which branch, and over, a cloth, impediment to the friend, in the position of that, her own surely omitted but not forgotten, so it becomes

impossible to point or to deny, hurrying into it, arranged along a path, the division between let's say heartbeat and thunder, or the alarm and Mahler's songs closing distance in, or the stones and paper waiting to be inscribed with the arrival at the circle as it curves outward

split open

to reveal

the excess of a dream, we who had been speaking mildly to each other following collapse, sipping tea in the tearoom, there, sequestered against those others and their meridians on the chart, it was difficult in this setting to notice, although the waitress was an actress, her lips scarlet, but this was only the lure of

glamour, toned muscles of the arm, cleft above the thigh. Found her
there again, again walking the horizon, where what was alive and what not alive
almost touched, as moments touch, walking now with her sister on the other side of
the line which is an illusion, the line, not the sister, she was there, among all the
sisters, their chorale in the meadow, now turning, now following the path

                                moving along the outskirts, crab-
shouldered, distended

                       her lesions unhealed, her heart, if she has a
heart, down to its stone, allergic to light and the casting shadows both, alert only in
the pitch and trill, the water under the edge seeping into foundations, drip by

             unable to find a glass

to peer

into or at the glassy contradiction, infinite regress
                                 drip
        beetles along an edge

as morning opens its envelope to find the newborn dead.

Meanwhile I will think a little in the middle. Think the day has a swan in it, long-
necked and idle. Think without the lingering kiss, its slight partition. Think
of the suspense of stages as you mount the stair, of the architecture spawned in mud
in a thicket of thorns, of how the literal squanders its chance. Think that the heart is
cut out of cloth and the cloth decorated with cutout hearts. Think how this would
lead to thinking about the heart's own factory

             or how hindered speech is condoned as appropriation, the
progress of gardens

off to the side.

     Think

as Haiti flames

                    or the sense that what was full is

spliced
so that air
rummages along draining familiar branches

ill-defined yet connected to a massive halt, cascade laminated, crowd stymied at the
fence, and the memorized agenda begins to falter and decay, heaved up along the
barricade.

Sleep turned to wakefulness, a kind of bag

                    carrying night's profusion, undone and missing parts of day
hauled across, partial tunes and burned flags, torn wrappings, murky waters, faces of
the newly dead masking faces of the newly born, the beloved loping at the crest,
pockets bulging with tissues, keys, and plans.

By morning the bag
broken, spilling its shade.

Thought that. *Nothing to say.*

The body, now light-headed and limp, an odd circuit, slight pressure, slight nausea
and fatigue, so it wants to curl up, sexless, lie down in the grass like a stone. A sense
of debris, nothing useful, scraps, leavings, odd dry bits, like the white mineral
residuum at the bottom of a kettle, bottle caps and pits and shreds of lettuce caught
in the drain.

The rebuke of mild air.
The rebuke of the following day.

It seemed a rival course had spawned a rival destiny from countermeasures and
hopscotch moves, players scattering into the woodlands and down the banks toward

the river, now breaking into chunks of ice. Beyond, blue-gray mountains spread along the haze, ancient sea beasts asleep on their rim.

And in the cavern where the dream reeled out, its images flickering on stone, the old hall covered with bright moss, courtyard wired up along its fence, and the sister unpacking pictures with new captions, and the boy tosses a crumpled twenty on the kitchen tile. Open on the counter, he reads *the lovers, the invalids, and the socialites* just before she opens an invitation

to join them at dinner immediately following.

        There were two cats, the one with a kind of staple in its fur, smallish and wild, and the other, already dead. And so the dead and not dead gathered in the building in the dream, the building also now only in dream, static in memory by day, alive at night.

Sound, what are you?

Over there

        slight

            nothing to say

happening now the full-take performance: sky roped in deep pink with purple interior crest *so what* like a down vest   smaller rodent clouds moving south train many dead in Madrid *so what* the long humped mountains soon to disappear behind the green spring green

     millions in Madrid in the pouring

  rain, faces

       black ribbons

         quietly in rain

denied

condolences from

a wreath

in Athens

nuclear biological chemical

dog units

beefed up

nothing to say

coincidence and chance   and now

pink

eased from the clouds   the rodents continue

south

headless, tail-less

and to where and to where and to

Dallas or

Moscow

or

New York.

Kill themselves for that kind of growth.

only
nine
hundred
and
eleven
days
later

millions more dream of owning

have a dream
the dreamspace
near the warmth of the fireplace

And the *final novel*

about to be truants   *local* truants.

On the next day we would look for the previous day among the remains, the red bucket collecting drops, body parts strewn into nearby fields of lavender, pages and stamps and words still fresh, recoverable, easily reassembled into anecdote and news. The constant mild readjustment of expectation or anticipation to retrospection, adjusting the narrative line to accommodate the slight or major changes that curve it away or toward, altering the end, which, of course, is not an end at all, merely a punctuation with a circle around it. And then it went this way. And then we followed along until we came to a sign. And then I said good-bye. And then you turned and I thought I saw you smile. And then he got out of the car and saw her in the crowd and called to her and whispered something into her hair. And then he raised the gun to the window and pulled the trigger. So not to shut the story down, close the book, to let the threads mingle into patterns impossible to dislodge without dismantling the whole fabric, and visible only in certain lights, at a certain distance

not anything
subjective *exploration,* objective *knowledge,*

position paper, letter, an exhortation to get beyond
habits of mind that keep

from staying within
these moments
at the level of sense to let it

rise up
         to include

what is forsaken or forgotten like the shells of sea creatures on the ocean floor that
are every now and then churned up and tossed out onto the beach to dry in the sun
and then be picked up by a young girl to put in a box on her dresser where she keeps
her collection. Some translucent gold the shape of a toenail and some opaque white
and some speckled like a flicker's back, some so small they are nearly imperceptible,
snails and whorls all the more perfect and wondrous for being minute.

From a distance, the ruptured train looked like a carnival, with the exaggerated
welter of vivid color and apparent disarray, ephemera as if cast from an exuberant
parade. The fact that the journey had been torn apart and the travelers sent off to
hospitals and graves could not be immediately seen, although soon enough the close-
ups of weeping relatives, candles, and draped coffins brought it to focus.
Nevertheless, there was a gap, an elision, between these images and their captions,
between the ruin of the wreck and the tidy inscriptions of representation, pictorial or
linguistic. We speak quite easily about broken hearts, but the image this phrase
conjures is never associated with bleeding, its literal content, because of course the
heart, broken or not, goes on beating just the way a clock goes on ticking

violence of chronology

        pressed into muteness
                coward and clown

as error migrates
terror into the terrain

blown open.

2.

In the film she is writing in a journal as landscape unreels

undated

We are in Rock Springs; between two boxcars I can see what is undoubtedly Main Street, with an attorney's office, an appliance warehouse, and a J.J. Newberry's. Long freight train; houses on top of a bluff. It has been weeks and weeks since I have seen a landscape that might be green! (The conductor just advised us that we are required to wear shoes while onboard!) Now muddy flats have appeared, but the color is still this grayish ochre, very pale, with darker tufts of what must be sagebrush. Passing now a field of mobile homes as the train swerves. The landscape closing up and then opening, flattening down and then rising in these peculiar dunelike shapes; one ahead has a sheer drop, completely straight, or so it seems from this angle. We are riding in tandem with a highway now. The sun lowering. The train quiet. We're in a sort of gorge, curving through curves. It is incredible, really, to imagine persons on horseback coming through here, and the Indians! Do I only imagine the sense of expedient squander this vista conjures; its human waste? Did Americans begin to develop this sense of moving through, moving across, moving on, because of the harshness and endlessness of this terrain? (White trucks that say COVENANT TRANSPORT *on them.) This cliff I mentioned earlier is now evident: impressive, roughly incised, reddish rock. The train is about to stop; I think I will get out and have a sniff at the dusty air.*

They come quickly, days
        and the ropes tied above
                        subject to doubt

where winter lay flat
and where bodies gathered like new flies on mold
and the big statements stretched across the
afternoon their gold

announcement
the spectacle greater than the small
occasions we might

recall
as certainly as the chat of birds at dawn
or even the explosions now

sequestered in our bodies

the sound of bubbles in a
pail
old leaves
inertia of frost
evening
surrounded by a blue frame
partly noticed, swelling up
a breeze from across the ocean, its empty shape
pressing on
shoulders

the mode of truth and the mode of peace

their inexact registers squinting up at the blank
no one can climb

and ghosts awaken, frightened that they are about to be disappeared forever, mere
slant light falling onto the table. Discrete yet slowly merging into each other,
shortly to vanish.

There is a leak in the kitchen ceiling from which water is dripping into a red pail
from time to time with a slight sound, rounded at the edges, so you can almost hear

the indentation in the surface of the water as the drops fall. Some of the drops are
not falling into the red pail, but onto the newspaper placed on the
counter under a second hole in the tin ceiling. The sound of this second
leak, more infrequent than the first, is muted and flat, *pff pff pff*

jet screams across the room

names of the dead in tiny print, in alphabetical order.

If I look closely I can see the sheened river through branches; as the sun sets, tiny
distinctions appear among luminosities, sky, river, car, white fence, yellow lights of
passing cars, pale stone of the graves—

horizon, eye—

As Dante, for example, chose Virgil.

3.

About life itself?
The search for water

a necessary condition
the possibility that life might once have taken hold

under some sun

you must have
liquid water

is looking for water
water on Mars

we know lots of

ice
at the Opportunity Landing

rocks
laid down

what can a rock
minerals in the rock

a specific set
the right temperature

a clue
a fingerprint

in these rocks
water that is flowing

The rocks were laid down.
The Martian soil.

Could we then be

unsettled

shifts in a child's toy
the Same reassembled

patterns of emphasis

unsteadily allied, but

now

let's move on
to the Living Legend portion of our inquiry!

No precedents!

The distorted stomp.
A cycle of songs.
A fictional small town.
Sing a song for freedom, sing a song for love.
You gotta move on.
I want to destroy the feeling that I am going to do it again.
I hate fitting.
I've been like this all along.
I was always happy to wear clothes that were out of style.
White bucks and red socks.
What were you listening to when you were young, Neil Young?
The bells.
Sensationally great and really beautiful.

Rain *plick plick plick* against the window.
The rattle of Texas chatter.

4.

To admire reason.
To be in awe of reason.
To think in a reasonable way about unreasonable events.
To reason with your enemy.
To feel yourself wandering from the realm of the reasonable.
To feel yourself flimsy within reason.

Begin again, after *Lear.* After *Lear,* reason abated, ebbed into nothing. Nothing but
we heard chimes telling and tolling, among what we said were intelligent faces.
Intelligent faces and the voice over the intercom a memory, and then the lights went
down. The lights went down, people appeared onstage and your purple shirt. And
your purple shirt touched my arm. My arm, in apposition. In apposition we had
moved toward the dictionary to test the ways in which. To test the ways in which I
slept and dreamed of water and a crimson thread around my throat.

Asleep after a pattern of *nothings.*

All this time had wanted to turn away toward
the altered coincidences of the near.

The man put up the building and then he died.

There are new blinds on the windows across the way.

To tackle certain things.

Nothing to say.

What is this?
Reason

leaps
onto unreason's

shivering spawn

      The man, his many
desires
the girl moves freely
between love and
love and

blackbirds and
she concludes, then, she
cannot live
without
blackbirds.

The room is ready, although no one is expected for years. Cheese out of the cold, crackers crisp, wine chilling. Pillows at optimum plump, floor shining. The best of the flowers, an assortment, arranged in a blue vase. It must be summer. When they come, it will be summer. Not late August when there is foreboding not of winter per se, but something other, a lassitude somehow connected to violence, like a slack rope around the neck of a bull.

In the film, a white face rides on a cloud of black, a sort of unattached mask, and it moved slightly at odds with the cloud as if they were part of separate, independent breaths originating in the minds of their creator. The black cloud had a mouth, but that was not interesting and seemed to be there at the whim of the plot. They needed something to eat something, and the poor hovering white mask was incapable, so they spawned a separate mouth in its garb.

If it were to visit, I suppose the mouth would eat the cheese and drink the wine, while the mask conversed about the weather. In late August, the storms brew up from the south, twirling destructive glamour.

Fox, quick enough to be almost illusory: you cannot quite know the space it inhabits. It marks a jagged desperate path and then leaps into the side brush. The half-moon appears in the color of the skin of a ripe peach, newly bruised.

Patience could improve your diction and perhaps your sleep as well. Never can tell. No point in the radiant suspended arc that sustains nothing. No point in sweeping the floor. Lifting the arm.
Lifting the arm up to wave but not to reach either the arc above or the path of dust settling underfoot. Blow on it.

Blow: the arc will disappear.

The Is Not That Is (Hélène Cixous)

What is *ist?*
            (hedgehog) (poem)
ellipsis evaluation
illegible thing   minuscule fortress
                  suffering
absolute singularity
to the other's keeping
that I am
a thing   name beyond the name *in a ball*
        animal thing
                        arrive *ist ist*
the hedgehog for example

Silkworm by heart   a ceremony
silk of self being of promises
                              bestiary
the hedgehog and the worm
wrap them up
        woman in her sorrow scarf
        blindfolded cathedral
        fragment of skin

Cat. Why cat?
Cat takes the time to live   (tact)   (humility)   (compassion)
Abraham the Ass   the inhuman exile   a creature of
inexhaustible creation   (guest)   (host)
Who is this?
                  Pardon me for not wanting to say
                              hanging in
                  air
                  it keeps its secret.
                  I apologize for not wanting to mean

not wanting to say
not making meaning

                       foliated hilarious even if secret

it is *ist ist*
what is not

the grandiose makes toys of us

when you are not ridiculous you are most ridiculous.

LINES OF FLIGHT

Unequal distribution   arbitrary float   Jonah in jeans
uncouth rampage Jonah in T-shirt *peace refugee*
and the dream with its wail
       implicit   forbidden salacious cool
         the dream always cool to wake to the cool heat of dream
retiring the name
              call it Jonah
                       call it the end of earth underwater

        call it the spider with her prey.

Cornered at the desperation of the field's disastrous unction
see how Jim might respond to Jim
Harry to Lavinia, Charles to Jane.
Or, in the redundancy of defeat,
Hercules might quit the team to join another.

Cold and colder still
instilled so that dream and not-dream coincide
as a nearly perfect coil.
What was his nervous antagonism? A name?
And what have you to say about these flowers
late in the season, so desperate and calm.
The whine of hope perishes
in time, just in time, for the jackhammers
to build an emblem science, and the small figures
to move in its midst like so many futures.

Dry Sargasso. The rash-lit arm, the virtual shoulders.
Tendrils of the chive and of the nodding leaf.
City I never saw
its music drenched
with journals and floating beds.
Lazarus, sky hewn among the dark boughs.
Dry Sargasso, its diary of husks.

Realm of Ends

1.

Francis turns. He has something to say. He has an
announcement. He says, *snow in summer* and falls silent.

A single egg in the nest. Francis turns.
It is not metaphysical; it is merely distraction.

Time passes. The nest is empty.
The snow, bountiful. A girl dedicates her last weeks

to a show of force. She writes gracefully about force.
Francis turns. He seems weak and small and without volition.

Thus the bird lands on his head.
Thus there are radiant seconds.

Is it reliable? Not the garden. Not the bed.
The streaming elocution is more or less prosaic.

The bird lifts up onto the bare branch.
The tree, an elm, is dying, almost dead.

Francis is indifferent but the bird, a cardinal,
shines on the barren branch.

Tit tit tittit tit hovers the weary pragmatist.
It is hoped, by Francis and the rest, that she

cannot know heartbreak, not
the melodrama of the nest's margin of error.

2.

All day in the fir trees, night remains.
Time passes. Francis is immobile, bereft.

He has recalled the condition of stone.
He has resumed his incalculable origin.

And so the second comes too quickly,
follows too quickly upon the first.

Others, mobile and incidental and lush,
attest to the perishable variety at large:

shark, polar bear, other political incidents
having little in common with the immobility of Francis.

A fence and an alarm, a cat and a cradle,
these also are not acceptable, not progression.

3.

The day has become abstract; I cannot know it.
It spits and complains as if it were real

but it is only a matter of time.
How, for example, forgetting

becomes opaque.
As if, dark on dark, an inert stone.

Francis is only a sentimental stone.
Francis is impoverished and mute.

Francis is a fiction of the glare, turning
into the Tuscan sun, under the juniper, among flowers.

Doves perch on his head and shit on his sleeves.
This is an example of natural observable fact.

Yet the day is opaque
despite recurring flags in the graveyard

lending their gala strophe to the forgotten;
despite the fantasy of the saint

turning in his soiled robes
under the heavy lemon trees, the ornamental

beds: rose, lavender, creeping thyme.
Along the path the lovers come

through the thrash of sunlit leaves,
the heavenly scents of lemon and rose.

The day is a tide of sensual foreboding
in the salty sweat of their backs

riding on white linen
in a luminous small room

in the taste of cool wine on their swollen lips.
The day, for the lovers, heaves with potential.

4.

The reverie stalks the real; it stretches abstraction
to its limit, deposited at the feet of Francis.

But given the impermanence of birds,
the cardinal's nest on the deck,

given the domestic and the spiritual
the utilitarian and

the forgotten, given
these cold mercurial shapes, arbitrary

hinges, islands, perpetual desires
and their advocacy among the least entitled,

given that one falls in love
with the condition of hope

and falls out of love with its
cruel replacement, hope,

so that what is valued is not the same
and the shape of the body in the window

is foreign, the picture of the woman,
her body and face

at odds with their person, at odds with her
curiosity, her pertinence.

In a dream of the girl and the lover,
now forgotten as the day, inevitably, is forgotten,

there is a difference between being forgotten
and being among the dead, but

given these episodes,
their proof turns to night and stone.

5.

The ears are ordinary, the feet
distorted. The girl has a condition

not announced in the greenroom
but nevertheless leaked to the press.

Biography has its compulsions, its regrets.
It could be the materiality of opaque gold

and the severity of promises,
their promiscuous gift,

oaths made on pillows between lovers.
There, in the eventide,

a strangling usurps the petty comma,
staggers from rejection to confirmation to murder

institutionally foretold. O Francis!
Do you stand for the cold, the cruel,

the bargain between such desire and such trust?
Take no prisoners. Let the homily endure.

The holidays are adept at the spectacle of divorce.
They specialize in silence, gala silence.

Masterpieces of the still life
make their way onto tables of the celebrants.

Holy! Holy! Holy! intones the priest.
Things are given and taken away.

Here is a token of my affection.
Here is my child.

6.

Turning the figure away, removing it
leaves its replica shadow

to shift with the gloating wind.
Later, the sculptor

pieces together poor bits of fabric,
copies from memory the shape of the lips.

The original remains vocable,
escaping the dream's

unscripted solitude, conceiving night's
blind, its familiar embrace.

Francis is silent. He has taken a vow.
Suffering unfurls its performance,

elicits revenge. On a ladder,
the man turns to address the public.

He imagines strangling the woman.
He speaks of his future in a nest.

After Tourism

Disturbed over her marvel I heard her say
something nocturnal I saw
mystery as merely change I saw
envy and the illegitimate mile I saw
under the formal atrocity at the messy embankment
all these and vocabulary lagging behind its science
tramp unknown soldier cop
talking strange talk
under an altered light under daze
I heard her say *tomorrow* as if she knew
I heard her say *come back*
and I choose you
as analogue of the yet to be.
Do not foreclose
investigation, but come along.
I will try not to protract my look into
now I will continue as if
you were next if you will I heard a man say
on the radio the other day, well, yesterday
talking about headaches
if you will
and today I had a look at
a Chinese cabinet only it is not clear
it is Chinese it
may be from another country I took
measurements nevertheless
for my next life I am thinking of requesting librarian
although I am as yet not on a list
of possible survivors I am

thinking of erasing the word *sorrow* from
the world, hurting under an illusory pennant
master of ceremonies hidden behind its junk
I am thinking of coming back as
part of your coat as a tree is part wind.

FIGURES MOVE (SAINT PETERSBURG)

Back from the thunderous *geist*
bills to pay, grass to cut, fish to fry.
The spectacle of tasks
importuning, scenes
folded under scaffolds of lore.

Figures move

collapse of particulars
reformation borrowed from chapter
and force.

VIDEO CLIP

Para enters, carrying Doxa,
aided by her friend, Lysis.

They live in the City of Ancient Signs.

Para is thin, very thin, and Doxa is heavy, quite heavy.
Lysis is listless, fatigued. She has been idle forever.

Under the Golden Arches they see a winged horse.
Lysis says, "Mythos."
Doxa agrees.
Para is fearful; she feels left out. She consults
Doctor Noid. Dr. Noid is annoyed with Para.
How many times do I have to tell you
to take your camera wherever you go?
How many times do I have to tell you
to record all events, sounds, weathers?
How do you expect the Real to return if you refuse

to obey these prescriptions,
to take these precautions?

Cat enters carrying an ass trophy.

END VIDEO CLIP

Morning cycles across night.
Almost enchanted by the light, almost annulled.
Were this the great bearing, were this merely
intrigue, or the architect's
confidence in the small shop of curiosities,
were the bride less stymied
in her great dress,
were any of these accountable
to the surge of one thing, one thing, one thing,
addition in space, bridge after bridge, and
the known but not recalled,
its bitter appraisal, singular
as the image of a girl,
long hair down over a shirt,
intent to be seeing, to be present,
she, the girl, long hair, open shirt,
writing something else.

VIDEO CLIP

Whim and Truce enter the frame.
They greet each other with a small bow.
Whim jumps up and down, hands overhead, trying to touch
the ceiling. Truce turns to leave, a trail of blood behind him.
Whim slips on the liquid and falls down.
Laughter track.

END VIDEO CLIP

Breathe deeply. Exhale whim. Exhale truce.
Can there be history?
Is it there, behind us in the park, Peter on a horse?
Is it in that cathedral, among the quick flames?
In Akhmatova's kitchen? In Mandelstam's death?
Can the Real return as history?
Ruin floods into images of new ruin and disappears.
Again! cries the child, *Again!*
Once upon a time.

II.

Down, down, down. Would the fall never come to an end?
—LEWIS CARROLL, *ALICE'S ADVENTURES IN WONDERLAND*

ALICE IN THE WASTELAND

Alice was beginning to get tired
sitting
with spring rain
on the bank
in forgetful snow. She thought,
It is too dark to see anything.
Then she began to wonder
about the meaning of anything
and the meaning of nothing
and in what ways *any* and *no*
were alike.
She said to herself, *I cannot see anything*
and then, *I can see nothing*
and thought they amounted to the same thing
and wondered
why two ways of saying the same thing
were needed.
If only, she began, and fell
asleep.

⁓

It is soiled, possibly bloody, the dark.
At night there are cries
of the suddenly dying: a rabbit, a hen.
The fox went out on a chilly night.
He prayed for the moon to give him light.
The tune leaked into the air like ink
into paper. In her dream, Alice
is falling downstairs
into a tub of words.

The thing is pushed
forward. It is cold, nonsymbolic.

So, nameless as, say, animals are.
Unless.
These stray *unlessnesses*
avert attention. They
give solace to it.
But it remains, a nameless thing
cordoned into consciousness
as if
being could withstand it.

The nomenclature of the
not living is
an it. *It,* said the soldier, torturing his captive,
it it it.
So let us have the White Rabbit.
Let us have this hurrying near.
Let us, among the
constancy
of living
and its
images
begin.

୬

I am broke! says the White Rabbit, hurrying to the
bank.
The White Rabbit, in the red,
has no redress.
Naked as a jaybird, the White Rabbit lamented, soon to be a jailbird.

But what is the color of chaos? Alice suddenly asked.
Gray, the White Rabbit replied, looking up at the sky,
like a sock.
But there are always two socks, and only one chaos, Alice said.
Colors and numbers are not of the same kind, answered the Rabbit
somewhat impatiently, almost knowingly.

How did you find a gray sock in the sky? Alice continued.

The cloud's contour, don't you see?

No, Alice replied. I see only a gray cloud, I do not see a sock.

But then, she added, perhaps I live in a gray sock, perhaps this hole is a sock into which I have fallen.

The White Rabbit disappeared as Alice was considering this possibility, so she was left without a rejoinder, in the solitude of conjecture.

Alice thinks something about eliminating the desire for revenge.

Alice was caught in the radiance of the not yet knowable.

This, she thinks, drifting, must be

the feeling of being young.

She could not say

in the radiance of the not yet knowable

which seemed, now, a reason for youthful sorrow.

⁓

Why do shadows get longer? Alice asked no one in particular. It must have to do with the angle of light, she answered herself, but this answer did not make her feel confident. The question lingered anyway and was added to by another. Does everyone know how to tell the difference between a shadow and a thing? The thin trunks of the trees had bent and crossed over the path.

Could one climb a shadow? she wondered.

Some can, came the answer out of the evening.

Who are you?

Who or what? came the answer.

Don't answer a question with another question, Alice said crossly.

Why not?

It isn't right, she said, not knowing why not.

A right angle, commented the Voice.

A right angel? Alice couldn't quite hear.

Yes, a right angel is something that can climb a shadow.

At that moment the shadows of the trees disappeared.

Alice continued down the path. She said the word *path* aloud.

She then wondered if a path was related to *pathetic*.
Pathos, she heard in the distance, somewhere above.
What is that? she asked.
A bear.
A what?
A bear, an emotional bear.
On that hill? That dark shape?
No, that is a shadow.
And that?
A bird.
What sort of bird?
An eagle.
I don't think so, said Alice. I think it is
a bunch of brown leaves skimmed by light.
The leaves flew away, their wings clutching the failing day.

Alice had spent most of that day reading.
It had been raining, more or less.
The book she was reading was absorbing.
It absorbed her, so she did not think about the rain
but let it fall on and around and beyond and outside of her.
The pages of the book became wetter and darker until she could hardly turn them
without tearing off a soggy slice.
When she finished the book, she felt lonely.
Why can't we see time, she wondered,
the way we can see space?
The book had carved another time into time.
That isn't true, she thought inwardly,
one cannot carve time.
No, but
perhaps, came the insolent, instructing Voice, one can *crave* it.

Crave rhymes with *grave,* Alice said after some moments.
I know, the Voice answered.
Alice continued down the path; she did not think the Voice friendly,

partly because of what it said, and partly because
it was attached to invisibility.
Are you a ghost? she asked suddenly.
Maybe.
If you are, then whose?
No one you knew.
How did you die?
I don't remember.
Alice was silent for a long time.
Are you in Heaven?
For response, a great rushing sound, and the tops of the trees
began to thresh back and forth as if violently weeping and there seemed
to be water pounding over itself like a huge crowd trying to escape
through a narrow hall.
Alice decided this demonstration was cheaply
cinematic and that she would not pay any
further attention, but would take refuge in
another book. She sat down under a tree and read:

April is the cruellest month . . .
She stopped and considered what an odd observation this was. Alice had thought a
lot about the idea that
some things happen because someone intended them to happen, while
other things happen seemingly free from anyone's volition at all.
She continued to read, hoping to find out why April is cruel.
You don't get it, the Voice said in a loud whisper into her left ear.
You are rude and abrupt, Alice snapped.
It isn't intent, it is a comparison.
What is?
April's cruelty.
A comparison to what?
To the other eleven months. It is like the unkindest cut.
You aren't making sense.

For Brutus, as you know, was Caesar's angel:
Judge, O you gods, how dearly Caesar loved him!

This was the most unkindest cut of all;
For when the noble Caesar saw him stab,
Ingratitude, more strong than traitors' arms,
Quite vanquish'd him: then burst his mighty heart;
And, in his mantle muffling up his face,
Even at the base of Pompey's statue,
Which all the while ran blood, great Caesar fell.

This speech sounded like a recording.
One cut out of many, one month out of many. The month, April,
is most cruel; the cut, Brutus of Caesar, the unkindest. Get it?
Alice picked up her book and continued to read. An orange
butterfly flew across the page, and Alice thought it resembled
an autumn leaf falling gently through the air's currents.
That's sentimental, commented the Voice, adding,
and sentiment is a failure of feeling, or pathos, as we were
speaking about earlier.
Alice decided to ignore this remark altogether.
The butterfly continued to skim the surface of the air. It seemed
a kind of breathing machine that made
silence visible. She read
. . . Breeding
Lilacs out of the dead land, mixing
Memory and desire, stirring
Dull roots with spring rain.

Alice found this depressing and inaccurate. She loved lilacs,
especially when she walked to the corner and saw them first at
the local Korean market. Well, she didn't so much see them as
smell them, and that changed the aspect of everything.
The land, she continued to herself, is never
"dead" but resting.
If you insist on this kind of truth logic, you will never be able to
read poems.
Alice shut the book. She found it distressing that the Voice could read her mind.
So the invisible gets to speak directly to the invisible; they are audible to each

other, and so the Voice is listening in, she thought, to my thoughts. She had learned that it isn't

nice to listen in on other people's private conversations, and so the fact that the Voice could

hear her talking to herself made her mad.

Don't be so prissy and pious, said the Voice, it bodes unwell for your future. You need to be flexible about rules. They change. Cell phones have changed the nature of what it means to listen in. Now it is a mere commonplace.

Yes, but you hear only one half of the conversation, said Alice.

Picky picky, the Voice responded in a high singsong.

Alice decided to change the subject.

Can you hear everyone's mind, or just mine?

I tune in and out, depending.

On what?

On whether or not I am amused. Of course, there is often severe interference, and your thoughts get mingled with others.

Really! This idea frightened Alice, although she could not have said why exactly. How many others?

Dozens, hundreds, thousands, the Voice said with a weary sigh.

What does that sound like?

The noise of history.

Do you mean you can hear voices from the past?

All the chitchat of the world.

In every language?

All. Plus the animals.

But you can't understand anything with that kind of racket, Alice said sympathetically.

I try to tune out, but it isn't possible. It's surround sound.

You need a remote.

Indeed. I ordered one, but it never came. They sent it to the wrong address, I think to Mars.

Mars? The planet?

No, the God of War. He always gets my stuff.

How annoying. Do you have a similar address?

Just then a siren went off, climbing slowly up and then slowly back down.

I can't hear you, Alice called. I've lost you.

Alice began to read again, but the words came out
confused and intermittent. Her mind interfered.

with dried
without pictures or conversations take the laundry in
over the Starnbergersee
what is that?
shower of rain   for the hot day   the pleasure of making
water the roses
in the colonnade in sunlight I have never seen a colonnade
of getting up   with pink
I hate pink
into the Hofgarten.

in that, in that
for an hour *Hofgarten*? Looking into the distance.

out of the way
on a sled
in the mountains
of the night
in the winter.

Roots, branches, rubbish.
At this time it all seems
unnatural
kiu

kiu
la la

༒

Alice gazed down at the ground, covered in wet multicolored leaves.
It had been raining leaves all day.

You probably should fill out a form.

Why?

Because by responding you will be disclosing to the merchant that you meet these criteria.

What criteria?

For understanding that which makes no sense for you.

What are they?

They are, for example, what crosses the path at the place of form.

Alice found this inscrutable. You mean if I walk along the path and come to another path that crosses it, that is where form is?

Sort of.

Alice walked on some way until she came to a path that crossed the one she was on.

I do not see any form, she said.

You are too empirical.

But I have no empire, Alice replied truthfully.

That may be, but do you have permanent interests?

Alice had lost the argument; it seemed to progress without clear incentive, like lightning.

What the thunder said, the Voice roared and then again roared from a farther place.

Wait, Alice protested, you are getting away from me. Can we back up?

Nothing can go in reverse, unless you are a machine, shouted the Voice.

I can retrace my steps, Alice said.

That is not the same as going back in time, which is nostalgia.

Nostalgia sounds like something for which you take a drug.

Nostalgia *is* a drug.

Jug jug jug jug, came a sound from the pond.

You need to study the difference between things as they are and things as they might be.

But no one can predict the future.

Pick a card, any card.

Before her, the landscape changed into a huge deck of cards swaying and floating, in radiant black, red, and gold.

Alice reached for a card and turned it over. It was the Ace of Spades.

As she did this, the other cards spun away, and she found herself standing with a spade in her hand, like a farmer.

Just then a Cat came out of the brush.

Alice of Spades, it said, and smiled broadly.

Now you are the most powerful card in the deck.

NOT! Came a roar. I am! I am!

The Cat turned slowly toward the chorus; Alice nearly dropped her spade.

Suddenly, a procession of Ings and Eens and Acks came forward, marching.

The All spoke at once.

I All-Powerful! I Anointed! I the Decider!

Put down your arm or I

will arrest you!

Pay no attention, said the Cat, it is only an army of benighted believers who think if

it plays its cards right, it will win.

Off with your head! shouted the All.

Fine, said the Cat, I have many lives to spare, and disappeared.

Off with her head! shouted the All.

Alice started digging furiously with

her spade and jumped into the hole just as the

All charged at

her, calling: Ready or Not! Ready or Not! Here All comes!

But Alice was far out of reach.

～～

One day, Alice is reading about another Alice.

What haunted her in this wasteland vision may have had to do with a sense of
deprivation, of there not being enough love in her own family to go around.

Does love have a quantity, like acres and dollars? How peculiar.

She imagined

a household with love moving outward

and not reaching the far corners.

This other Alice lay in the unloved space

like a discarded doll.

Why, she wondered, do people lose interest in some things and not in others?

They die, said the Voice dryly.

You again.

Have you lost interest in me?

I think so.

You think so? You think enough to know or not to know so.

Thinking and knowing are not the same, Alice said.

In fact, she added bravely, thinking is almost the opposite of knowing.

Don't be pretentious.

I am not pretending, I am thinking aloud, and that is the way I come to know.

Then thinking, in your view, is a prelude to knowledge?

Prelude is a lovely word, Alice commented.

Is it?

Yes, it has a feeling to it, as if in the uncertainty of things there were a mysterious beauty, as if only one instrument were playing, only one bird singing.

Dawn?

Yes, the dawn's early light.

No comment. Do you play with dolls?

Yes, I have many of them, and I make them do things and say things.

Did they always agree to this doing and saying?

Of course. They have no choice in the matter, since I am the one who is playing.

Do you play with soldiers too?

Girls don't play with soldiers.

Why not?

A doll was on the floor, facedown.

There was a rip in her arm and another on her ankle.

Alice had wrapped blue bandages around both these wounds.

Because soldiers take orders to kill.

Just then a huge limb of a tree fell to the ground, making a terrible thud.

The Voice, now far off, called

And sport no more seen
On the darkening green.

⁓

What, Alice wondered, is the difference between
adventure and *dementia*? They

sound so much alike.

Not really, the Voice replied, at least not so as I can tell. It's only that
middle syllable, the
men and the *ven*.

Bob Dylan makes those kinds of rhymes all the time.

Who?

He's a singer.

Never heard of him.

You will, Alice said dryly.

I'd quote you some lines, but permissions are prohibitive. I suppose
I could sing to you
and then no one would know. She sang.

Bugs illumined in the setting sun, minute integers of life.

◟◞

As she went along, Alice felt
the heavy gate of night close behind her. She
wondered if it were locked, and if
she would ever
find her way back through it to daylight. Ahead,
she could see very little.

She lay down on the damp ground and looked up.

Stars pulsed like tiny flares reflected in a sea, illuminating nothing.

Everything is suspended but changing, she thought.

She pulled at a damp blade of grass.

Nowhere-never droned around her
and blew on her skin.

A spray
of notes, or motes, issued into the air.

A nervous watery breath
lifted stray hairs
and set them out on the grass.

Perhaps, she thought, I am dissolving.

She began to hum. The Moon appeared,
exhaling a trail of thin cloud.

I am glad to have your company, Alice said.

And I am glad to have yours, answered the Moon.

You are entire, Alice said with a trace of envy.

It was ever thus, answered the Moon glumly.

But you wax and wane.

Yes, wax and wane and wax and wane ad infinitum. Nothing changes.

But everything changes, depending on whether you are only a thin curl in the sky or a great luminous ball.

Changes for you, maybe, but I remain the same, a monocle staring down while the sun comes and goes.

But the sun doesn't move, you do.

Whatever, said the Moon. You go around the sun and I follow along like a dog on a leash. Without you and the sun, I am a paltry gray rock.

It is a terrible case of codependence.

You have very low self-esteem, Alice said. Everyone here thinks the world of you; you are always mentioned in poems and songs.

I know. It makes me cringe with shame. Moon this moon that, lovers and moonlight, nocturnes and sonnets. It's a total cliché. Stick an *r* in and you get *moron*.

Alice stood up, casting a long black shadow.

Look how tall I am!

I will never be tall, answered the Moon, and disappeared behind a heavy cloud, erasing Alice's shadow and sending her back into the total dark.

An owl *hoo hooed* from a distant tree.

Alice felt afraid.

What's it to you if I live in a pit?
What's it to you if I cry?
What does it matter if I never get fatter?
What's it to you if I die?

What's it to you if I fall in a ditch?
What's it to you if I'm sad?
What does it matter if I never get rich?
What do you care if I'm mad?

This ditty seemed to come from nowhere.

What do you care if I'm far off or near?
What's it to you if I'm weary?
Does it matter at all if I'm caught in a trap?
If I'm a lunar moth or a fairy?

Alice spun around and fell down.
I do care! She cried, I do!
Is that true? You do?
Yes, tell me where you are.
I am here in your ear.
In my ear?
She touched her left ear.
Ow! Ow!
Sorry, Alice said. What are you?

What do you care if I'm a flea or a gnat?
Or a very small, excellent spider?
I am not a mouse or a rat
and I don't know what rhymes with spider.

That is called an exact rhyme, Alice said.
Is it now? How?
Because you used the same word twice: *spider* and *spider*.
Just then a bluish light, no bigger than a drop of water, flitted in front of her.
You're a firefly! Alice exclaimed.

Firefly! Firefly! burning bright
In the forests of the night
What immortal hand or eye
Could frame my fearful symmetry.

You're stealing from Blake.

It's not a mistake.
I'm a terrible fake.

I'm jealous of his Tyger
always burning brighter.

All I do is come and go—
I'm all illusion, not much show.

You and the Moon seem to be equally dissatisfied. You should be glad to be such a
magical luminous creature. I have no natural light.

You have turbines, and ignitions galore,
I'm only an intermittent spark of allure.
I come on for an instant, neither bulb nor orb,
a mere flitting mite with a poor dim light.

As it sang, the firefly moved off into the distance.

Good-bye, I must fly!
Want to come?
Alice and I
make a fabulous twosome!

Alice wondered what the firefly might mean; was she meant to race after it? Already
it was only a blinking spot in the dark. But then, in a rush, she found herself beside
it, hovering.

O my, am I flying?

Flying thou art
in a fit and a start.

Come, come away
before the break of day.

Alice wondered if she was still Alice. No one will recognize me now, she thought. I am one among many and we are all the same. Everywhere she turned, she saw mirror images, pulsing in the dark just as the stars pulsed above. She realized she knew nothing about the life cycle of a firefly and wished she had paid better attention in biology. She had always wanted to fly, ever since Peter Pan, but this somehow was different; she was stuck in another story the ending to which was not knowable. I'd rather be reading than being a story, she thought.

Reading and being do not rhyme.
You'll have to do better if we are to be on time.

Where are we going?
I hate not knowing.

Just follow after.
Let's head for that rafter.

Directions are scarce,
our map is my trace.

Let's wake up the swallow,
he can sing us a tune.

I'll lead, and you follow—
late and soon.

I'm breathless and scared
and your rhyming is forced.
Now it is Wordsworth's
The world is too much with us.

Little we see in nature that is ours.
But now, you see, we are one with its prowess.

It's *powers*, not *prowess*! What is your name?
My name is the same as the wishing game.

Make a wish double fast!
I wish I were Alice, cried Alice.

Alice rhymes with *palace*!
What fun!
Better a palace
than a barn!

Everything that happens is a word.
That's absurd!
Not if you're heard!

A Peacock appeared then with radiant plumage. It cried its terrible cry and Alice remembered *I remembered the cry of the peacock.*

Why do you cry?
Because I am so beautiful.
I ravish sight with my azure eyes.
And we all weep together, a hoard of captives.
I am the palace and the prince.
I am the enchanted and the enchanter.
I am the end and the beginning of each day.

Then the sun came up then.

Alice was not sure if her wish had been granted, and if it had, by whom. She could not see clearly in the early light whether she was still a winged bug or a girl. She felt lonely and cold in the damp dew. Beside her, she saw a strange netlike thing hovering in the grass. It looked, she thought, like a handkerchief dropped by an angel, immaterial yet visible. Well, she thought, I am still thinking, so I must still be Alice. The sun began to make the world sparkle around her. The handkerchief glistened. She reached for it, and as she did, it vanished.

That night, Alice dreamed of cheese, proper names, an elevator, a sad child, and mistakes. She had lost her address and, since no one was expecting her, she felt a kind of delirious freedom at the same time as she felt totally alone. She dreamed that she saw a man she knew, and he stared at her blankly.

She dreamed she was in a tall building that swayed in the wind.

⁓

What are you reading?

A poem.

Does it rhyme?

No.

How can you tell it's a poem if it doesn't rhyme?

For someone who listens in to the world's conversation, you are massively ignorant.

No need to be insulting. Enlighten me.

Alice was silent.

So?

I'm thinking.

I know that. So far your thoughts are inscrutable.

It's like love.

What is?

You know a poem is a poem the way you know love is love.

But love is more likely than not an illusion.

The feeling of love is not an illusion.

This is not a good enough explanation.

Poems don't need explanations, Alice said, and added in her sternest, most grown-up voice,

and if I remember, you are the one who told me not to be empirical, and now you are asking me to explain something that is not within the bounds of explanation. Poems are examples of themselves.

As in, I know it when I see it? Without an objective criterion, you sink into mere opinion.

It has to do with how words vibrate through more than one sense, more than one moment. Alice wished the Voice would leave her be.

Read to me.

Alice read.

⁓

Do you have a name? Alice asked one day as she was walking toward the river.

Yes.

What is it?

I was christened Goggle, but most people call me Gog, I think because I seem to be the same coming or going. I'm not really capable of making distinctions and I am without a direction.

Then you aren't human.

I thought I had made that clear. How many invisible humans do you know? Many, but most of them are in books. Your name, for example, is in a book by Samuel Beckett.

He took it from an earlier source, the Book of Revelation. Here it is direct from my favorite source, which, by the way, I invented:

In the biblical Book of Revelation, a power ruled by Satan will manifest itself immediately before the end of the world. In the biblical passage and in other apocalyptic literature, Gog is joined by a second hostile force, Magog; but in the books of Genesis and Ezekiel, Magog is apparently the place of Gog's origin.

Are you evil? Alice asked. The question itself made her heart race.

Evil is as evil does. It is an interpretation, not a condition. It isn't innate.

But what exactly are you?

I got caught in the crosshairs of brain and technology. It was a crisis, or crux. So I am neither one nor the other. That's the reason I wouldn't know a poem if I fell on one. Just then, the Voice stubbed its tongue on something.
Damn! said the Voice, it's the Weather!

The wind picked up, blowing a few last leaves across the ground.

Alice wondered if, when she is old, she will be wise.

Is wisdom something that comes naturally, along with gray hair and wrinkles? Is that old woman sitting on her porch wise? *Wise* rhymes with *eyes,* so perhaps wisdom is a way of seeing especially clearly, like a clairvoyant. *Madame Sosostris is known to be the wisest woman in Europe.* What a silly name for a wise person, Alice thinks, not
like Athena, which sounds wise. Athens must be named for her, but a city cannot be wise. Madame Sosostris is reading cards and she says:

I do not find
The Hanged Man. Fear death by water.

This sends chills through Alice's soul.

Who is the Hanged Man?

Alice saw in her mind's eye a man, with dark eyes and hair, and another, in a mask, placing a kind of scarf around the dark man's neck. Then the masked man takes a great thick rope and places it around the dark man's neck. The rope turns into heavy coils. The dark man looks complex: resigned, intelligent, amused, hidden, cruel.

The Moon was in eclipse. A shadow passed across its face. The Cat was looking out on the snow seeing something Alice could not see, even if the Moon came out from behind the shadow. Someone phoned and left a message. Alice thought about the idea of an answering machine. It seemed an odd idea. A machine would always say the same thing, no matter what question it was asked.

Are you there?
Are you there?
Are you there?

The *you* of the question was not the *what* of the machine.

The place of human action, Alice thought, has moved off and left behind only actors wandering among broken, leftover sets. The Moon, in shadow, was part of a set.

The tracks in the snow, the greenish sky, the single star: sets. Someone would come out before long to sing a song of longing. What, Alice wondered, is love among machines?

Sappy, the Voice said, and dated. Get real.

There was a silence that filled with ambient sounds.

At last, Alice exclaimed,

I know what you are!

O?

Yes, you are a by-product.

A what?

By-product, a sort of leftover from other processes that left you, like ash after fire, or slag after the copper has been removed.

I don't think I like that idea, it sounds even less attractive than *recycled*.

It is. You have no further use. You're an end in yourself.

Another silence.

Watch out, said the Voice, you are in danger of thinking us both out of existence.

∽

When Alice woke up it was still snowing, a fine, salty snow that moved like a veil in the wind. For some reason, she began to weep, and her tears turned first quickly to icicles that then as quickly melted, leaving almost invisible tracks. It was impossible to tell the time, since the light was almost uniformly a gauzy pale gray in which the darker trunks and branches of trees seemed to be suspended. But for a cardinal that tore a fresh wound through the air, and a few dark hairy hemlocks, color seemed also to be almost gone. But none of these things had anything to do with Alice's tears, which seemed to have come from a far-off source, so remote and unknown that they felt like those of a stranger. Perhaps these are not tears at all, she thought, but only the melting snow. But her eyes kept flooding from within, and the tears kept breaking over their lids like spill over a dam. She wondered if she were crying because of something in a dream. She could not remember her dream.

In the smudged air something stirred.

What ails?

I cannot say. It is as if before.

Yes, as often. Mine, also.

Before?

Aye, another time, when there were violets.

There are violets now.

These sang among rocks.

Singing violets?

They belonged to the winged.

Winged violets that sang?

Spoke also as they lay down along the path.

The path to where?

It was not to anywhere, it was from everywhere.

O.

Aye, a sort of O, an ambit.

It is snowing.

Aye, the O is caught inside of the snow; it is in pain.

Am I crying because of that?

Perhaps.

It seems strange to cry for an O.

It isn't for an O, but for entrapment, for the fact that it is caught in snow.

Once, it was my mouth.

Your mouth was the path from everywhere to nowhere?

Aye, it was the news of awe. It was the scandal of Omission and the law of Oblivion. It was the Overt sign that filled itself with nothing, leaving all else Out. It was an Ocean whose spoon lifted the whale from its Origin and poured out its Oil into the hot gold lights along the bridge where the lion roars.

I once saw that bridge.

But did you hear the lion roar?

No.

Do you hear the cricket?

Yes.

Can you describe the difference between the sound of a lion and the sound of a cricket?

I cannot. It is ineffable, outside of the linguistic index.

You cannot point at it, nor to it.

No.

My mouth once could say the difference between the lion's roar and the cricket's song.

By mimicry?

No, by coming from many places and going nowhere.

Then your mouth was not entirely for sound?

My mouth was the route through which sounds pass.

So is mine.

Aye, but your sounds all know where they come from and to where they are going.

The snow is like fog.

The foggy foggy dew.

She wept, she cried, she pulled her hair.

Air trapped in *hair,* as the O is in *snow.*

The only only thing I did that was wrong.

That was then also.

With the winged speaking violets?

Aye.

Alice watched the birds in the snow. Some were dark gray with flashes of white you could see only in flight, and others a tawny brown; some were tinged with a yellowy green along their wings while still others wore small black caps. Many had delicately woven stripes and stippled chests. She knew some of their names— chickadee and nuthatch and finch and song sparrow and tufted titmouse. A pair of mourning doves huddled on a bare branch of the hawthorn tree. Before the snow came, robins had begun to appear, and she worried about them now, wondering where they were and how they could eat with the earth snowed in. She wondered how these names came into being: robin, titmouse, nuthatch, finch. They do not know their names, she thought, and yet they seem to know each other. Knowing their names and being able to describe them is insufficient and meager; these do not bring me closer to them.

The tricky ordeal of words. They are elastic frets, bringing us closer at the same time as they push us away; we think by naming things that we capture them but this is a ruse, and you see how we are trapped by it, trapped in use. *Ruse use us.* Every word contracts and exfoliates thus. Folded into each *core,* an *ore.*

Everything must come from somewhere.

Thing, where, every, some. Mine, alas, from the undone.

Your ore?

Yours also.

What is the undone?

Not a what, nor a where, nor a some. Yet still, a sum.

Many?

So many.

More than how many?

Whatever your count, more. The stars and the non-stars, plus: always, the sum plus one. A call, indifferent and dangerous yet without even a trace image, horizonless, unstacked. The faulty implosion and aftermath of sight which is why, here in snow, I return briefly. I cannot be remembered, so do not be alarmed. I am merely the eternally Open, as in the portrait of the monk's mouth, into which and out of which time pours.

What you say is impossible.

Aye, also contaminated. The numerical is a dungeon. The murderers are there, counting and pondering tomes and licenses, always counting, counting. They breed, although they have been unsexed. They return as blame.

Alice sat in the snow, watching the March birds, the grackles and juncos and tits.

Only if I am invisible, she thought, will the birds stay. If I materialize, they will fly off because they fear me, except it isn't me, Alice, they fear, but the ways in which I am not one of them, not a bird. There was no way to assure the birds that she had no intention of hurting them, or of persuading them that it was she who had scattered seed across the snowed ground.

Why don't they connect these two facts? she wondered. What the birds knew was of another conceptual order, one in which her intentions and her actions were forever severed; she could not argue or protest; she could simply remain trapped in the difference between what she was and what they were.

I am real but unknowable, which means I cannot be actual and the ways in which I am real are confusing; perhaps, she thought, I am merely a memory or a dream. What if the birds are actual and I am not?

The wind made a hollow whistling sound; the trees swayed.

I am insufficiently present, Alice moaned, and began again to weep. She was beginning to suspect that she was not really alive. She was beginning to suspect that she had no parents but that instead she was a kind of mutant guise or emanation with a proper name, itself quite common, that had innumerable places of conception. There was Alice James, sister to William and Henry, and there was Alice B. Toklas, friend and lover of Gertrude Stein. There was, of course, the Alice who wandered around in Wonderland, for whom she had been named, the creation of Lewis Carroll who wasn't really named Lewis Carroll, and he had named his Alice after a real little girl named Alice. I am an effect, she thought. I am a mere motif at the mercy of someone else's pleasure, someone who thinks by pretending that I am alive she can make the birds comprehend something beyond their existence, but she is wrong.

Even if you are not real, said the Voice, you can be true.
Alice started.
I don't want to talk to you, she said sulkily.
You may have no choice.
Maybe your battery will give out.
Maybe, but that will be only a temporary cessation, like a cup of tea or a trip to the bathroom to pee.
The snow is melting.
Don't change the subject.
What is the subject?
Your truth as opposed to your reality.
O really, she said, and slipped into a nearby wood.
Following her, an incomprehensible jargon of something found in the jumble sale of Language.

As like is cadence-repetition exists
as living is contributing either

a literature its creates everything
a language internal chance enchains
a linguistic Idea concepts encounter
at least in combines espouses
a longer involves carries encounter
apprenticeship lost in close either
at libratory in confronted elements
and lives itself covering external

The next morning, when Alice woke up, it was spring. She could tell not only because the snow had melted away, but because there were alterations everywhere; under the sodden leaves of fall, minute beginnings: dark reddish nubs and bright green kernels just above the surface of the softening earth and, on the thorny rose stalks, tiny furled nodes; the squirrels were chasing each other, performing impossibly acrobatic swirls in the tawny grass, and the mostly silent birds had begun to sing.

It must be April, she thought.
Aye,

Whan that Aprille with his shoures soote
The droghte of Marche hath perced to the roote,
And bathed every veyne in swich licour,
Of which vertu engendred is the flour;
Whan Zephirus eek with his swete breeth

What language are you speaking? Alice asked.
English.
But I don't understand most of the words.
Aye. Language changes. Words morph and disappear into the mire.
Mire is an example. What is a *mire*? It rhymes with some sad words, like *liar* and *dire* and *ire*.
The mire is the wet ground, swampy, like a bog. It came to mean *to be in difficulties*.
Like getting bogged down? Alice said.
Exactly.

Sometimes I think language is as beautiful and mysterious as nature, and no matter how much we learn, it never gives up all its secrets and surprises.

To this sudden appraisal there was no response.

Hello? Hello?

Two boys rode by on bicycles, calling to each other in loud boy voices.

⁀

Alice was sitting in the grass. Around her there was a scattering of small buttonlike yellow heads on slender stalks, nodding slightly above the grass.

Dandelions, said the Voice.

I know, Alice said.

How did they get this strange name?

Etymology can help you there; you can trace a word from its origins. It isn't a dandy, not like Fred Astaire, but the teeth of a lion, from the French *dent de lion,* and before that, from Latin.

Alice was silent for some minutes.

She was trying to make a connection between a lion's tooth and the soft yellow heads of the flowers.

She found no link at all.

It isn't the head of the flower, Alice, but the shape of the leaf, which is serrated like a tooth.

The Voice roared with self-congratulation.

Alice felt equally edified and annoyed and changed the subject to something the Voice couldn't look up with such alacrity.

Is a dandelion a fact?

No, it is an object.

Objects are not facts?

That there are objects called dandelions is a fact.

I see. And their color, yellow, is that a fact?

Yellow is a color, an attribute, not a fact; but that dandelions are yellow, at least until they turn gray and lose all their hair, is a fact.

Alice took this in. It seems to have to do with sentences.
And things that happen, are they facts?

Not exactly. Events find their bearings by a kind of extrapolation; out of all the possible relationships between and among the particulars of the perceptible world—the dandelions—we construct events—they are hinges between the immediacy of the present and what went before and what comes after.

But that isn't quite accurate, Alice said, knowing that by contradicting the Voice she was asking for trouble and, indeed, the wind began to pick up.

Events are in time. But the way you said it, it sounds as if we make events up, whereas events happen that we have no control over. Earthquakes and storms and terrible accidents on roads, for example.

As Alice made this observation, the crowd of dandelions nodded and swayed excitedly.

You are talking about stories, I think, Alice went on, getting up from the grass and walking quite quickly up the hill. She thought a storm was in the offing. But an event isn't a story; stories add event to event, as if stitching them to each other, or putting beads on a string.

Event horizon! the Voice shouted.

What?

Event horizon! The edge of space-time! The great maw of the universe!

There was thunder to accompany these bald statements.

I am not looking through anything, Alice said disconsolately, and whatever I say is not seen, except in the mind's eye, whatever that is. So far, nothing is as it seems or seems as it is. Really, I would prefer to be a cat and trot along with a bird in my mouth, its head hanging limp, feathers listless.

Being a cat is nice, said the nearby Cat.

I grant you that. Being a cat means you can go from violence to affection without any discernible transition.

I kill, I purr, I eat, I sleep.

These are excellent variations on a theme of being alive, if not exactly sentient, and I recommend them to you as a cure for your humanness.

But I like being human, Alice said, and then added, sort of.

And besides, I haven't any choice in the matter.

But of course I am not exactly human, she added, I am a fiction, which makes things more complicated on the one hand and a lot simpler on the other.

However, said the Cat, you are the emanation of a human, so that makes you more human than not.

No, Alice said, once again feeling disconsolate, I am only words.

This is a bare fact and there is nothing to be done about it.

But Alice, said the Cat, are facts not also a matter of interpretation?

Perhaps you are not mere words.

Alice was silent for a long time, long enough for the Cat to clean its face by licking its paws and then wiping them across, first one side, then the other.

O I don't know what facts are, Alice said at last.

Once I thought a fact was a thing, substantial and irrefutable, like a table or a penny, but now I am not so sure.

I know facts have something to do with evidence, she added, since the Cat had said nothing in response to her outburst.

When people say what the facts are they seem to be saying something about reality.

The Cat wandered away into the shade of a rosebush. It had lost interest. The Cat was not interested in either facts or reality.

Alice went back to her book. She wished there were someone wise and informed enough to help her with facts and reality. If that person appeared, then, and only then, she might be helped with the more awful problem of truth.

∽

One day, Alice was leaving CityCity on a train.

As the train pulled away from under the tunnel of misgivings

it passed a message on a building:
IT IS NOTHING TO YOU, ALL WHO PASS BY
What a strange thing to say
to the passengers, Alice thought,
It is nothing to you.
What is nothing to me, to us?
On the way back into CityCity, she saw the sign again.
Is it nothing to you, all who pass by?

—*to Willa*

III.

The romance of the precise is not the elision
Of the tired romance of imprecision.
It is the ever-never-changing same,
An appearance of Again, the diva-dame.
—WALLACE STEVENS, "ADULT EPIGRAM"

Echo Revision

1.

Lest, forgetting, the branch-maiden lopped off.
Lest, forgetting, the branch-maiden lopped off.

Lest the rotund silk, flickering on a wall,
Lest the rotund silk, flickering on a wall,

Nagged by wind. Prose
Nagged by wind. Succulent prose.

Swift enough to roll downhill into the stream
Awake enough to roll downhill into the stream

(Violent, or gentle, naturalism). To claim
(Violent, or gentle, naturalism). To claim

Our attention, like soldiers, or:
Our attention, like soldiers, or:

Not like soldiers. Not like soldiers.
Not like soldiers.

And the apples and pears assembled on the white cloth
Apples and pears assembled on a white cloth

And the couple under the enormous tree—these
And the couple under an enormous tree—these

Picked out details on a chart. Then
Picked out, paused. Then,

Stumbling out from under the enunciated dirge
Stumbling out from under these forms

Of twilight's last screen
Sudden hatchings, partitions, reversals.

There were several hatchings, several namings,
The lesser and the leftover piled up

Several reversals of one into more than one.
Over the fecund industry

Had there ever been such magnitude, such spawning?
A counting of cast-off limbs.

Such counting of last limbs on the green?
To have unreason counted as reason

To have as fact unreason without crime
And only one intentional wound; to be

To covet the black eyes of the small dead rat.
Covetous of the smallest wakeful hour as

Adding and adding so the agenda grows
Of the black eyes of the small dead rodent.

And the blood stops running, the scar sets
Adding and adding so the agenda grew

The scar set and the tune rose into its thin retainer.
And the blood stopped running, and the scar set.

The scar set and the tune rose.

2.

A modest evocation, a simple claim. As his crimes were disbanded
A modest evocation, a simple claim.

At his death, the mourners came out from their foxholes
As his war crimes were

And the crows also.
Forgiven at death, the people

The year turned into another year overnight
Came out from their kitchens

The day turned into another day overnight
To mourn; crows agitated the air

The war was a separate entity, with its own turning dates.
And settled on kill.

The candles were lit.
The year turned into another year overnight.

Nevertheless, candles were lit.
The day turned into another day overnight.

Some counting was included in the dossier of events
The war was a separate entity, with its own turning dates.

Counting seemed to ease the ambiguity of the ocean.
The candles were lit.

There are the pluses and the minuses to add and subtract.
Nevertheless candles were lit.

The issue of fewer or more. The issue of cost.
Some counting was included in the dossier of events.

But, turning away,
Counting seemed to ease the ambiguity of the ocean.

The innumerable and the inseparable
The issue of fewer or more. The issue of cost.

3.

And the incommensurate
But, turning away,

In their separate, unique garb of silver
The innumerable and the inseparable

Riding up and over the long radiant angle
In their plural garb

Like a flushed stream of mercury
Rode up and over in a long radiant angle

These seemed to make the weapons and their procedures useless
Like the flushed stream of memory

Blank came back, blank followed blank, until full.
These made the weapons and their procedures fertile.

The pathos of the hour, its desire to be spoken.
The pathos of the hours, their desire to be said.

Noon came and went and no one watched.
But noon came and went and no one spoke.

No one watched, heard, or was beseeched.
No one watched, heard, or beseeched.

Know me! called the empty bell from far off
The two hands reached up, surrendered.

And swiped its card, and drove away.
Know me! someone called from far off

And the couple stood and kissed under the boughs of the tree.
And swiped his card, and drove away.

And the old man smiled to the camera.
The couple embraced under the boughs of the tree.

The old man, now dead, had smiled to the camera.
The old man smiled to the camera.

The young man, a soldier, smiled to the camera.

THE SCALE OF RESTLESS THINGS (FRA ANGELICO)

1.

Error bloom
inadequate   spent

all the odd gloves thrown away   subtract the G
            nothing to retrieve   add   C

                        cloves

                                    array

                        unverified
                heat twisted wind
                    mistaken for favor
                        merge
                        lift up

                    pluck from vertigo

the shack's
bravado
swept out to sea.
Save the *O*.

                            Dripping
                not blood, not water,
                    refuse of light
            metaphorical
                        distension beyond the immortal If.

You might know how everything names itself as cost

84

and the poor
the shotgun shack

not water, not blood,

not yet conceptual
as if
          to ornament the sign
                    as easily as a
                              strap
as if
in the welter of the exiled new
the girl
                    ripped slip and no hair
she, too, had been shorn
like, and like an image.

2.

Enter in an initial *D*

The Devil in monk's garb
the first hermits

a ring of space
around the head

miracle of the Book
floating across fire

knee-deep in mud
dream of the puddle

dream of the cloud
floating gift, missing

arc of the halo
and a lily

enters the pattern
blue figures on the roof of the hut

central pinnacle
missing also

long vertical drops
architectural

3.

        The puddle is bitter.
        It tastes of shiny
        coins. Notice now how the lovers,
        reflected in it, are
        warped to perfection.
        A chickadee sips and bows and
        sips the moony bowl.

        The mercantile dressage at the core of the Rose.

    Enter in an initial *R*

surrounded by a frame
where the minus conducts business partly noticed
    a breeze from across

        scatters the miscellaneous *N*
      and the trials of Islam   call of truth and
        call to prayer

           their inexact registers—

In our story, how Abelard spoke
and how a crew migrated over the plains with its primer of elision
the treatise on hunger
on imminent foreclosures of the real—
fury in stasis
black dog returns

and the past flips up

as if
word of mouth
could resurrect the simple course of seasons
sitting on the porch could save the world.

4.

If the saints were to meet
If the apostle were to call forth the magician

If the falcon were to reveal
If Francis were in the fire

If the palpable ordinance
If the wallpaper were singing

In replay she awakens.
In the wake of the replay, she
is awake. It was
all a dream.

The century in which she was a boy,
the hugely upholstered dress,
the pretend attraction to the swarthy lad.
If you
blinked, you missed it.

If you
blinked, you would have missed
the moment that she wakes
awakens is awake.

Almost an object of sight, almost
within bounds of the known
a new age
new tusks   new furrows
new starving rats
new mildews and rings   new illuminated Spiders

bright berries on branches catching
ochre leaves   there are no images

5.

Nevertheless
belated in affection   *I*
had gone   goes   more or less has had
to cede moist residuals—
unkempt sheets, etc.
The modern furniture, a cool polyester gray
out on the curb. And yet,
the materials, acquired,
cheat their source.
Moved away.
Moved toward.
Moved, or turned, away.

Flirty filmmaker deceived *I*
and her ancestors, soiled her
party dress, whipped her torso,
led her across red rope at the club.
Made nothing *absolute* happen,

as she stepped away from a better job.
This is a *full-service* enterprise.
This is gutter and candle,
the informant and the slain.
Outrage, a kind of rash on her face,
on the grainy silent screen
as the director's mirror breaks open the sea.

6.

In the film of the painting,
the zip zips open,
dust flies
through the opened edge
the yellow fringe
the crimson tide

                              leave expression behind

mimic and aura condemned

                              and so

open the miraculous envelope.
Read the blank page.
As usual, some German angels
spread-winged, are faced to the past.
As usual, one of them is sleeping.

7.

I launched a scroll
in the misgivings of January,
after Rome. As *I* began

writing to the beloved,
something went awry.
"And so" I explicated the loss
and earned a degree.
I watched the escalator rise,
I mentioned positions and hats.
I kept the heart girdled by fact
so that desire and its
accompanying historical grace
filled the auditorium with scholars.
Sleeves, *I*'s sleeves, swept over the podium.
The field, *I* said, is infested.

Have you seen the orchid man?
Have you seen the blue eggs?

Prefab symmetry
lost its magic, its surfaces

purloined from drugstore
polish. *I*

sets out to mesmerize
having lost, having never found

the blue eggs.
If you catch the light, go.

She might have called it
a fool's error

            the collector
         crossing his arms
             directing traffic away
                 from what *I* might have said—

Did you see? Have you seen?
Infidelity of the page.
Bug specks on the mantel.
Body parts, etc., on the field.

8.

The mess, the empirical debris
already written
in swank pretense up in the old hotel.
We gave him some money for new books.
His shoe had a hole in it, we could see that
as we walked along the road.
We speak of the person whose
words fall through the sole of his shoe
onto the muddy path.
For new *boots*.
Error, a splash across a hem or cuff.

I is in the theater
where *I* will create
the main character.
The audience is assembled
has assembled will assemble
its hosanna.
The man his wife the young man
the rumpled sheets the man
the long kiss the touch
the man his wife
her sweater. The luggage the visit
the young man his embrace.
I is in the chamber of birth.
The chorus explodes hosanna in the highest.

9.

The dream's deception.
The companion moth.

The cold child's fluorescence
masking its source.

The lover
sitting on an immense blue egg

in a nest of light.
Smile for the camera

dear herald, dear
avatar, we're not sleepy and—

Perhaps it was only the decorative
jewels of reason's promise

spoiling our outlook
the prismatic gems

the geometrical clasp
glinting on her neck.

No blood on the cutting room floor.
No ashes on the mound.

Uncharitable hard moments
of the architectural swerve—

bring back normal boredom
bring back the philanthropy of the Golden Age

bring back the sorrow of a single loss.

10.

How went it?
Covetously.
And now?
Also, but dead.
How goes that?
Sadly.
In what manner?
Mercurial, somewhat imagined,
certainly no longer.
A train?
Also.
Gambling?
Evidently.
The small ones?
One by one.
Smoking?
Yes.
With love?
Now and then.
And so?
And so.

        The hour going on   it was it was
the little nerve pain at the side of the head

the dream from hell
and her bedside reading might be

how numbers are not time and time
is not

singular
what a friend said

at lunch
is it hot enough

in the minimalist cave
is it cool enough

in the cave of modernity
in the studio of the artist

in the preening hello/good-bye of the good old days
so not to be inward, to be outward and onward

with the iPod attached to iTunes
all the numbers in play.

Alone in Open (Bill Viola)

Into the trees, over water
      saturated trellis
          the body midair

            catapulted beyond daily weather

         ethical event

     those villages

                    a simple man of
                    the people
                    ordinary people

                    the healings

dust and spit
the balm of storytelling
performing miracles
        Augustus

           and a Jewish peasant
                his teaching, agrarian
                  loaves, fishes

              multiplication's

rustic enigma

                    mustard

kingdom of mustard   the seed

        Rome or god or prophet or maybe

thousands

the tokens of their deliverance

everyone killed

someone is going to kill this man

looks for a target

make edges

treads, turrets, defines the features

filter

lenses

filter

this energy using this mask hot

spot on a camera marked off

with this cross

the key

high altitude loiter

a strike element

accuracy of the Patriot

hard to stop

merely conventional

or

or

40 percent   or

basically a failure

Silkworms   guided

anchored off the coast

to the ship
a sea

to conduct
continuous

escape
after these whitewashed tombs

after the war

                                          new narrative New

the trauma
hearts and minds

so different
to himself

up to the year
what does he say

and to whom
meet the women

go and tell
the last scene

                  the story began

                               I did not expect journalism

                    very early
                        the stories

six hundred troops
Agony in the Garden

exactly what
happened

on a different day
before the beginning

so here's the scene
all the lambs slaughtered

and the Lamb.

Untitled (Gego)

Touch
were there any
was there a flotilla
or, arguably, was she
standing on nothing
untitled obviously

the drawn harpoon
the rigorous crowd

forms of sway
articulated stoppage

after the multiple descent
the Nude's catastrophic joints

                          down down down
                          abysmal sight

              the drag on her knees
              the stiff drumbeat

nothing at which to point
arrest of the hovering craft

punctum abrasion silt

inexplicable gap
surprised to be standing
pinions of optical shift
what was said   *at passages.*

Sometimes I think we will
perish just there
under that sign
at the appointed time
when nothing points back
so that what is held
is exactly not
between this *that,* that *this*
in the traffic of hours
the knotted cage
where nothing is kept
the hinges of hope
thin coordinates
matter as shadow
fossil imprint
untitled light.

CONSTELLATION IN CHALK

These ready-mixed colors are available only in
case of emergency, dial
power
with one arm showing
green, then orange flashing, then green.
An airplane? Plane of content—sleep's sound
harvests twenty stamps, each with
floral arrangement, and poison
merit, ultra in the night,
the drawing on the left
a creature in want of wings.

The Third New International
harbors a bug roving, its minor journey
neither in nor out, where the pointing is.
Sandpiper below Essex, Park,
their finish three stories above a hollow noise.

Door hauling.

I would like

five red apples, please,
but omit the five and the apples.

This was an episode in description.

Morning's adapter came without
messages from the near—far near, only
mobile structures, flanged and muddy,
mind spooled at the knot, counting without measuring,
a topography of cost scratched into the floor.
Rug slide. Box shapes, and moist smoke
leaning on the environment

like an Idealist colony speaking in tongues,
climbing the hill in period costume,
bothers, sisters, before we hear what was said.

Record of records, the paradoxical mouth.

On that side of the river
a ghetto bus replaced the high orchestral cloud,
rose to ragweed, field with visual noise,
the elders' parade
dragged toward the crows' damaged carillon.

There was a splinter, or leak, in the habitat of selves,
more names than things on the
stage. Only the recording had remembered
and it was shard. *I paint what I paint
said Rivera.* In a dusty window, a sad-eyed doll
caused one to point as at a final moon, an
instrument long surpassed: thought-ghost reads the *fi*
the *fa,* child invents, sighs, scribbles
outside the faint stance of the ready-mades.

How much is that? One or two themes
slink away, scented in derision and
the decision not to play.
Tendresse mystery genre whose fast horses
and arcadian themes
question the robed dawn. *Hehe hehe*
as careful as a ladder leaning on air, nonsense chapters
drawn onto the figural ground.
She swallows the poison, waits and counts. Psyche's
pool of omission reflects the flying horse as the villain leaves
his semen card in her body of reams (operatic ring of gold).

She draws the Empress from the
deck, its familiar headdress of snakes, one for each
known dead. Nobody's diary, somebody's curse.
From his niche in the anthology the Hero speaks,
eyeing her bloody or painted toes, her livid mouth.
Strip the prayer from the kiss web,
it is merely sham. Salvation has undone
her eternal soul into little itinerant drops,
each younger than dew.
The moon's strap slips off the shoulder of night.
Night of Nights it is called; all must follow.

In memory of Barbara Guest

Elegy for Sol LeWitt

The weather map today is pale. The lines on the map
are like the casts of fishing lines
looping and curved briefly across air.
The sky now, also, toward evening, is pale.
On Sunday, in Beacon, there were lines
drawn on walls and also lines
drawn across the canvases of the last paintings
of Agnes Martin. One of them has two pale squares
on a blackened field.

              The lines on your walls
follow directions
as if

as if there were a kind of logic
charged with motion
at the end of winter: the pale blue northern cold
almost merged with the pale green
at Hartford, and then the blank newsprint of the sea.

OR TO BEGIN AGAIN

1.

Way over in the particularities of evening
so many missing it seems we are alone at
last, you and whatever I am thinking about you,
not a happy thought, but not indifferent.
And that other world? The image
had receded under the angry claims of the
image, and in this redundancy
we stopped to buy apples, and to speak of the dead.
The face of the dead came into view
as a consolation, and the apples seemed
a magnitude of form, brightly gathered, a crowd.
These are impossible things to say clearly, because
the proper name has less than accurate
attributes: so little had been copied from life.
But think now of Seurat. Think of *Child in White*
rendered as absent agitations of a crayon. The end.

2.

Or to begin again
gold touches the back of her neck. It spawns
a crest, a brief tattoo. She moves
into and beyond
shedding its improvisation, its effect.
The effect of gold is bright heat. She
seeks cover in a passing cloud, a passing leaf. Gold
moves off into the landscape, touching a wasp, a truck,
a stone. Down at the end of the path, a head
appears as that of a man, riveted to a wall.

The gold moves off and vanishes
as night ignites a halo
around the head at the end of the passage.
This is the assemblage of *nevertheless,*
its sudden rupture. I thought of something else.
I thought of a stranger seated in a tent. The end.

3.

Or to begin again
I had wanted a location but had become embattled
in a zone of supposition and indirection.
The emergency is ink-stained.
A temporary orange blocks the view.
An ambulance is climbing slowly uphill.
Returning to the lost, the sound increased
over whatever exemption had been founded on passage.
Around and around they went, the metallic children,
carving an arena into the climate, an
erasure that would become a road, repeating the turn,
learning its rhythm in the denuded wood.
He began, "I sought, this time, to approach him."
I thought then of the witness, of the carriage of the
body moving downstream on a barge, and the small
red tug like a living toy, riveted to its mass. The end.

4.

Or to begin again
in the miraculous scale of the small nouns,
their mischief and potential.
Auden imagining war at a sidewalk café.
Oppen staring into the face of a stranger,
into the face of his beloved Mary.

We want to be here.
I was thinking of table settings: folded napkins,
polished ware, sparkling glasses.
And the prayer? What was the prayer?
What if everything had slowed
and she had chosen to wait, to forget her chore.
There were, I recall, ripples of violence
that caught on twigs and snapped wires.
Words were spoken from too far away to be heard.
There was a blind spot, a stained cloth. The end.

5.

Or to begin again
suspended above the habitat, bees
dying in their boxes, salmon
desiccated in their nets, flight on flight,
origin marked by tracks in mud
and the river newly revealed
through naked bark
like a silver coin skipped across time
the migrations of time
the small noun time.
The world fallen from its skin
into the airy wild, abode of infinite
contraction, this in which it is, adhering.
A swarm and a nub, tumbleweed shadowed on ice.
The facts encroaching on intimate constraint.
These could be a hand, a voice. The end.

6.

Or to begin again
an accident disperses the law. Thrown there,

there. Less than forgotten
in the usual ditch of leaves, weeds, caps,
a massive gold afloat in the autumnal sky.
At whose approval? The call stuffed in a sock?
The faces of the war dead in a signature farewell:
boy, boy, boy, girl, boy, boy, girl,
picturing evidence, picturing silence,
and the chorus ready to respond: *holy, holy, holy,*
to awaken the dead but not in the language of the dead.
Perhaps a finite contraction,
the child practicing to fly overhead, to drop the bag
on the dusty road below, to watch it spill into flames from on
high, from a mobile perch
cruising through its episodes of grief. The end.

7.

Or to begin again
some got lucky, came rushing
toward the giant appeasement of the given.
Singing along with the anthem
they distributed coupons to the rest
to redeem, solace for those who do not
begin but stay back in the infrastructure
of the singular: what you said, what I said, before
the fact. Were we to be among those to be counted
one by one, like days? Greeted by our host?
In which language? And what were we meant to
carry away, down the road a bit, into the rest?
Light strays across the dry grasses.
The arm lifts, the head turns.
A gathering, an image, a dispersal
in whichever order. The end.

8.

Or to begin again: *now now*
birdlike, repeated,
the noise of nearness,
yet without either body or mouth.
In the mind's eye, a wall
painted robin's egg blue
behind Paul Klee's dirty yellow circus.
Nothing noticed, nothing gained.
A clown on his head, a dog, a ball.
And yet the acquiescent rain,
and yet the passage
of a massive chant
through the fictive pilings of a cage.
Comest thou now? Comest thou now?
Repeated, birdlike, from over there.
Look up and then look away. The end.

9.

Or to begin again: virtuous moon
appears to be taking a star for a walk; I
cannot see a leash, but the star
is obedient. Together they traverse
the night sky. It is winter
and the ground below is a dull shell.
The secular ghost is chastised
in its moody camp; it fears ice
as it fears the dawn when the moon
will have vanished, star in tow.
It knows when things begin to melt
there will be a forgetting and, in the wan face
of the beloved, the stigma of desire.
Fuck desire, says the ghost, only

no one can hear and so no one can answer.
Fuck desire, it repeats, birdlike, at dawn. The end.

10.

Or to begin again: a gift is in the offing.
Something a sparrow might drop
on its way, something sent
across the boundaries of time.
Why is the deck at a tilt
so that the day and its objects
might slip off the edge? The boy
with the fiddle, his
dark brows flat, eyes recessed
into the harbor of play:
four strings, taut bow, the arc
of elaborations, note by note, his wrist
traversing their wake.
The day has its spelling, the night also.
Tell me what she heard in the splashed instant.
Say the last kiss. The end.

11.

Or to begin again—still no sign
in the field of negation.
All appears to be ordinary.
Seabirds depicted above the sea,
the pretty couple dancing,
the buzzing saw,
evening clouds assembled, mountains dark.
Yes, but the page is not blank.
Yes, but the sun's pallor
consumes as it rolls

across the heavens, dragging
the head of the beheaded despot,
the embattled fishermen
combing the sea with nets,
the girl with a dove in her suitcase.
I had wanted to count the steps. The end.

12.

Or to begin again having quoted, inscribed,
having changed a few words
along the way, a gesture toward
the gaps between is not, is, is not.
Eve gives me a map traced on thin paper
with a red dot. The boys walk along the road,
their hoods up, their speech riddled.
The red dot is where they were headed
in the year of the snake. We decided
against perfection. We said
perfection is a morbid
judgment against the living.
The girl with red hair was imperfect.
They did not come with only a suitcase on a boat,
Eve said. The Dutch, I said, made paintings
of nature arranged as perfect death. The end.

13.

Or to begin again: thisness abbreviated:
margins, earshot. Have no herald, no scope
under such bearings, only an instruction
to carry on under the new doctrine's law.
A friend is known to speak
about the difficulty of understanding.

Could he climb higher to see better
as from the distant star
occluded beyond ever knowing?
Now obey this.
The steps lead nowhere, so only
the small bird, hiding under boughs, escapes
the mirage of escape.
Fidelity ruptures at the core
over there, where he hurled
his oath at the corpse of belonging. The end.

14.

Or to begin again: lavish permission,
ribbons placed back in their bag,
pulled through the sleeves
of the prisoner's coat, the suicide's
gun. The Arab men
are playing backgammon in the courtyard.
The preacher's voice fills the chapel
with iconographies of faith.
Our tears turn to ice
and the mourners stop along the path,
informal now, unrestrained, makeshift.
So that with nothing held back we sigh,
beyond time, for that green pasture where time
stands still. Does not. Does. Go back
before the beginning, before
a promise was made. The end.

15.

Or to begin again: chronicle of thaw
and the sitting hawk

and the tilting stones.
The place has become
a saturated edge
moving quickly along the road
up over the arc of bridge, flag, sun,
and the hanging man. Fact
dissolves into fact, proximate to
the slowest economy, the most forbidden dream.
The girl enters knowledge.
You can see her on the trail
of the smallest bug, the most inglorious weed.
We join her in the aftermath of promise
where she is studying the tides.
World without image dilates. The end.

16.

Way over in the particularities of evening
gold touches the back of her neck. It spawns
in a zone of supposition and indirection.
Auden imagining war at a sidewalk café.
Origin marked by tracks in mud.
At whose approval? The call stuffed in a sock?
Begin but stay back in the infrastructure
nothing noticed, nothing gained
as it fears the dawn when the moon
recessed into the harbor of play:
the head of the beheaded despot
judgment against the living
the mirage of escape
stands still. Does not. Does. Go back
where she is studying the tides.
Go back to the beginning. The end.

In memory: Katherine Mester Luzzi

Ann Lauterbach was born and grew up in New York City. After college (University of Wisconsin, Madison), she attended Columbia University on a Woodrow Wilson Fellowship, but moved to London before completing her MA in English literature. She lived in London for seven years, working variously in publishing and arts institutions. On her return, she worked for a number of years in art galleries in New York before she began teaching. She has taught at Brooklyn College, Columbia, Iowa, Princeton, and at the City College of New York and Graduate Center of CUNY. Since 1991 she has been Director of Writing in the Milton Avery School of the Arts at Bard College, where she has been, since 1999, Ruth and David Schwab II Professor of Languages and Literature. She is also a Visiting Core Critic in the Yale School of Art. Lauterbach has received a number of awards and fellowships, including a Guggenheim Fellowship in 1986 and a John D. and Catherine T. MacArthur Fellowship in 1993. She lives in Germantown, New York.